It's Right Where You Left It

Theo Martins

NOTE TO READERS:

While the thoughts, examinations, poems and anecdotes in this book follow a loose narrative, the chapters can be read independent of that order.

The QR Codes enclosed within this book can be scanned with your phone to listen to the chapter's corresponding song.

www.theomartins.org

TO
MOM & DAD

Mom, thank you for showing me the limitless possibilities of this life. You breathe life and color into everything you do. Father, your skepticism has impressed upon me on greatly. Thank you for your bedtime stories, they have provided wild fuel for my imagination.

CONTENTS:

CONTENTS:

PREFACE

As a child I journaled often. My elder Sister held notebooks full of journal entries in her room and I knew because I saw them. I've always written and enjoyed the submersion that would occur when I read. I could visualize the sentences in powerful ways and I loved when writing shook me to my core. I understood it was my fascination with how the words lay on a page than the book itself. I do not consider myself a writer but in crafting this memoir I realize I am. The answers point to the details I recall and the manner in which I convey them. When I look at the span of my artistry writing is the source from where it arises. It is the foundation I have built my imagination upon. I do not write to educate or inform, I write because it is what I am designed to do. I write to free myself from the spell of nostalgia.

I've tried everything that my mind believed it needed to get to what I believed would be the end to all worries. And when I reached what I believed was the end was another incline. This is not what I wanted. But while I fussed and fought with this discomfort deep inside I enjoyed the fight.

I felt freer from it. I took pride in the scars left from the experiences and began to observe familiar patterns because of them. It has been a journey of going up and down the mountain. I have arrived at the understanding that this is all there is. I have conquered my mountain but it is merely a blip in a sea of mountains. I have learned that it is best to presume nothing and that the could be's and should be's are clever attempts to distract from the reality standing before me. It is best to pack light, most of what you need you already have.

This memoir is comprised of examinations, poems and anecdotes that stand as a reflection of the accounts that have led me back to myself. If it was indeed right where I left it then at what point did I decide to leave it, and why? How did I know what was left and when did I know it was time? These were questions I had to know. My accompanying self titled debut album is the manifestation of the answer to those questions. Everything I was looking for was right where I left it. I am grateful to everyone who I have crossed paths with, shared experiences with and have spent time with.

PART ONE: PARENTING AS A SPORT

SAY HI TO THE TOUR GUIDE

I was so engulfed in the tour that I forgot there was a tour guide. Someone had introduced me to this world and the absolute enjoyment of it fueled a deep sense of curiosity for where the source of it derived. There has to be a well from where this comes from and I must find it. I have looked everywhere, I have explored everything within my grasp but it did not measure up to that feeling. It did not last. On a trip back to the east coast to I realized it wasn't the state or the town I grew up. It was inside of my home and it was *them*. Not only was it them, but it was what emerged *from* them. But how?

My parents lived opposite lives. My Mother, a devout Christian, my Father, not interested in faith. My Mother floats and dreams, moving as the inspiration decides it should. My Father, frank and practical. He maintains the same job he got when he arrived to the United States. He does not take vacations.
Somewhere in between the contrast of my parents lay a mysterious crack in the door. A door of choice.

And I saw it. And once I saw it I could not unsee it. The sight of that door and the wonder for what lay behind it sent my mind into a tailspin. It was as if I could not shake it. Through every job and every experience it was there, quietly sitting in the corner of my mind. I tussled with it, ignored it, fought it and have walked away from it. I did everything I could to block the urge of what this stirred in me. But when the pain of reality came knocking I immediately recalled that door, wondering if it still lay open. It did, just as I had left it. I thank my parents for what they've cultivated. In their individual choices lay a unique path.

I recently mailed each of my parents a note to thank them for being my sole inspiration. My Mother, responding incredibly casual, "of course, son. We love you". My Father, frank as expected, "you're welcome". In that moment I realized that it was my revelation and not theirs. They were aware and they basked in the freedom of that understanding. You can hear them both on the outro of, "Love Me Sometime".

My mother called in the middle of the song's recording session to say thank you and I taped it as I often do.

Scan To Listen To
"Love Me Sometime"

PARENTING AS A SPORT

My Mother was Phil Jackson. The winning for her came when her players achieved. That's what she's there for. My Father was the team owner. He didn't show up to games or press conferences often, but he made sure the lights stayed on and the dinners were funded. And that was a mighty job because there were a lot of players on the team.

DEVOTION

My Mother attends church every Sunday. She does not miss it. Weeknights after returning from work she would watch Oprah, make dinner and head to her bedroom for an hour. "I'll be in my room praying. Don't interrupt unless it's an emergency.

If your Dad calls take a message". It was common for her to take space. Always. And I did not understand it. My Mother's love is unconditional, there is not a time I cannot access it. She loves her children and it is felt in every waking moment, but there was one thing that stood in between my Mother and everyone else: her time of solitude. Sometimes I would test the strength of that barrier. I'd crack the door open and ask a feeler question, purely to see how she'd respond. My Mother wouldn't even reply. Quietly knelt by her bedside I could hear a low hum, sometimes with tears in her eyes. This barrier was impenetrable.

It is my Mother's devotion that I have imbibed. Her devotion to her faith gave her limitless power to draw from. Had she relied on the skills that define a Mother she would falter when things didn't work in her favor. It was as if she knew there were other forces at work, forces that mortal hands couldn't possibly construct. I don't subscribe to any faith or practice other than the desire to understand the Truth about all things, but it remains clear: I am the product of my Mother's devotion.

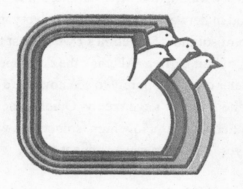

SUNDAYS AFTER SERVICE

Every Sunday while my family attended church service my Father slept in. He wasn't asleep he just lay in to avoid the conflict with my Mother who prefer he join us. An empty home on Sunday morning was my Father's time of solitude. When we returned from church, music would be on and food would be made. As a chef, preparation was my Father's specialty. Sundays after service was my favorite. I knew my Father was in a good mood when I heard the sound of music from the driveway. The smell of stew and rice met me at the front door. The energy was electric. I knew my favorite uncles would likely stop by and if they came I would be in for a fun evening. I never wanted those Sundays to end. My Mother was devout in her faith and my Father devout in his freedom to choose, but seeing them unite on this day gave me joy. We would dance the afternoon away. Requests for money were granted on these days. Any problems I had at school I told my Father on these days. He would simply smile and nod as he danced in circles, surrendering to the joy of the moment. As the sun began to set so did my Father's mood and I hated that. I wanted to do anything to keep the energy up, to keep him happy. But Monday was soon calling and the demands of the weekday sobered him.

Music lifted him. It gave him a moments freedom. And I had to have that freedom, not just on Sunday but forever. My Father is a tinkerer. He worked on cars, wrote doodles on the back of his bill envelopes, played the trumpet and was the family DJ. He was a track runner, soccer player and great swimmer. He was a postal man and nearly applied to become a fireman. He won the heart of everyone. While my Mother played the rear during social occasions my Father's effortless cool took center stage.

On a family bus trip to Houston he brought a cassette tape of music to listen to. I sat beside him and he placed headphones over my ears. It was the first time I heard Hip-Hop music. It was a mix of sorts that included Pete Rock & C.L Smooth, Digital Underground among others. When I became a DJ my Father and I clashed over what we deemed was "good" music. My Father didn't enjoy the curses on songs, he felt it ruined the essence of what was being felt. I was fascinated by the freedom of these artists to curse. What attracted him to Hip-Hop was the Soul, the grooves, melodies and harmonies. The same grooves he would play in the music of Fela Kuti, King Sunny Ade and Shina Peters. My love of music and groove comes from my Father. The connective tissue in the grooves he found in Juju Music, R&B Music and my discovery of it in Hip-Hop formed a unique marriage

of sounds. I had not yet understood but this became
the foundation in which my sound was influenced.

CHURCH

I grew up going to church. My family attended a
nondenominational Christian church. It was
predominately White and the music reflected the Soft
Rock ballads of the 90's: acoustic & electric guitars,
electric keyboards and drum sets. Going to church
everyday Sunday was a concert. The church
community was a big family and so the invitation to
play music was always offered. My Mother and
sisters joined the dance ministry, I preferred to watch.
I was intrigued by the musicianship and watched their
every move. They strummed, slapped and plucked
these metal objects with such ease. They were rock
stars. One in particular was Kim Clement. A
musician, prophet and frequent visitor of our church,
he would come seasonally to perform and he was
loved by everyone. He commanded an audience. He
genuinely enjoyed singing and I could tell. Sweat
would drip from his long hair as he would transition
from the piano to his microphone. It was different
from the countless pastors and musicians that visited.
As a DJ I became aware that the power and influence
of music lived beyond the confines of church.

I saw the parallels very clearly and they were no different. There was an audience and there was a musical guest. The church offers a tithe for the guest, club owners pay the artist a walk through fee. Churchgoers believe their way is separate of any other faith, clubs use VIP ropes to designate the important from the unimportant. In their differences lie a clear similarity.

PRAISE & WORSHIP

My songwriting structure came from attending church. The use of guitars and refrain came from my upbringing attending the nondenominational Christian church with my family. The build up, the sustain, the refrain came from later teenage years attending a Pentecostal church. Then as a DJ, cultivating an understanding of what I like and how to convey that to an audience. All of that has been a case study for making music. If you look at the structure of the songs on my album they follow a very natural guide: simple refrains, 1-2 lines in constant repetition, a focus on the use of words. It's a method that I learned naturally growing up in a church. Church worship focused on the choruses, they would build the song up, pull it back, build it up again.

I spent much time looking for a reason as to why I make music and there is no reason. Like church, it is born of a pure desire to praise & worship. I make music because I can. That is a celebration in itself.

BEDTIME STORIES

My Father read bedtime stories to my Sister and I as children. He would arrive home from work still in his uniform smelling of cooked food and sweat. I loved it as the scent enriched the stories he told. These stories were never consistent. He would improvise as he went along, often inserting a parable of obeying your parents and finishing your homework. I was aware of the improvisation but I loved every minute of it. We got to experience this story together. This was ours to keep and ours alone to share. This gave birth to my love of storytelling.

BY THEIR SEEDS

"You will know them by their seeds", was a line my Mother would often say in regards to any moment that she felt it suited. It essentially means that if you want to have an understanding of something watch what it produces. I liken she meant it in terms of

actions but I view it through the lens of observing to understand. My family had a dog and her name was Joy. She was a Husky Labrador breed with salt and pepper fur. She was incredibly friendly. My Mother picked her from a litter of puppies and named her "Ayo", which translates to "Joy" in Yoruba.
I was not as close with Joy as the rest of my family, I preferred our relationship be casual and not close.

We lived in walking distance from my former High School. Everyday at 8am and 3pm kids would walk to and from school, laughing, running, dribbling basketballs and sometimes running onto our lawn. The disruption would send Joy into a frenzy. She would run up and down the stairs. She would jump on couches and incessantly bark until not a single sound of a teenager was heard. In those moments Joy was not the friendly dog I knew.

It didn't matter who walked by, she barked. And barked. And barked. It was only when she was let outside to see the passing children did she become silent. The fear of the unknown. The drastic and reactive measures we take with the potential of harm in mind. Most of the conflict within my family had been born of fear.

A fear of not understanding. A fear founded on an untruth. Whatever we feared wasn't real, but it was simply the fact that there was something to fear that kept conflict in reach. Conflict, for many, is just as good as company. In Joy I saw our fear, because we raised her.

NO IS NO

My Father would often get on me for not completing chores. I hated chores. My job was to vacuum the house and clean the bathroom. Our old vacuum did the opposite of vacuum and I did not want to clean bathrooms. I waited until the very last moment to do anything chore related. "I never have to remind you to eat", my Father would say as he saw me in the kitchen one evening. "I was busy", I retorted. I explained school was taking my time and I needed to study. This wasn't exactly true but he wouldn't argue with school. "What about before school?". I paused. I didn't have a response for that. He walked off. I stood in the kitchen exposed, a hole poked in my flawed perspective. I knew then that I didn't like the feeling that accompanied an excuse. If I couldn't do something because the circumstances were out of my control that was one thing, but failing to keep my word felt beneath me. It was hiding for the sake of hiding. My Father always kept his word, even when he said "no", it was always no. A gentle but firm man, charismatic but solid as a rock, I revered the aura that grounded him. I respected how solid he was, how as much as I demanded of this role I imagined of him, he didn't step beyond his limits. In the space that lie between us I learned the truth.

RECOGNIZING A PATTERN

Every Friday I would join my Father as he ran his errands. He would pick up his paycheck from work, grab parts from the automotive store, deposit his check at the local bank, head home and prepare for his work shift that evening. Every Friday. On one Friday during our trip to the bank my Father went inside to the banks ATM. I followed him as I was bored with sitting in the car. As he walked up to the ATM window he gestured to watch him. He casually selected a non-English language setting and proceeded with the inputs to successfully to receive his money. I looked at him in confusion. I didn't understand, how did he do that? He didn't speak the language he inputted so how was he able to get what he wanted?

The questions weighed on my eyebrows. He could tell and replied with a grin. He never explained how he did that, but I never forgot that day. Home curfew was 8 pm sharp. Unless you worked or had permission you had to be in the house by 8 pm. My Father held no compromises about that. Because I was a working DJ I was required to be out as late as I performed. Sometimes as late as midnight, other times 2 am. This was the ATM experience I had with my Dad as a kid and even he hadn't noticed. The point of entry was different but the results were the same. This was the start of recognizing a pattern.

Self Conflict

PART TWO: LED ASTRAY

I've been led astray by my thoughts.

Thoughts that have formed habits.
Habits that have formed patterns.
Patterns that have created rules.

Rules that have given rise to the riptide of emotions.

All from a thought.

But who's thought, I ask?
Where did the thought arise?
And Why?

How do I know what I know to
be true without knowing what is
not true?

Why does it matter? A voice replied.

The wave of emotions recall a distant feeling of familiarity.

I have been here before, I said.

But where? The voice replied softly.

I've seen this before but in another.

I've shared this moment before but with another.

How? The voice replied.

Again, I do not know. I do not.
But the feeling has not left me.

LED ASTRAY

WHY I LEFT

The truth lies in the quality to understand something. One could see a tree and say its a tree. Another would see the same tree and describe its origin, the season it blooms and the fruit it bears. It's the difference in stating what something is and understanding what it does. The former is just memorization, the latter is an understanding of how it works. I knew what my Mother believed of me and I knew that my Father named me, but that was the extent of knowing who I was. In understanding something you become free of the complications that arise from the lack of understanding. You can refine that understanding to the degree of how free you want to be. This is why I left home, to understand.

But understand what? Understand the feelings that stirred in me. What was that feeling? Where'd it come from? Are my friends feeling the same way? I wasn't sure but I had to find out. There began my start. My weekly trips to New York gave glimpse to others who were also on a similar path, but there was no way a group of people felt the way I felt about this thing.

I grew up in a house with 6 other people and while we were extremely close we each had very different interests. I would speak to these friends candidly about my feelings and the responses indicated that the only person that could get me to where I want to go was me. It was time to put that to the test.

I soon moved to Los Angeles. An opportunity arose and I knew if I didn't make a move now I would regret it. I told my family I'd be visiting for a few months, but I was lying. I said that to ease the reality of what I knew was happening. What I yearned for was the freedom to fall. Sometimes the love of a parent can be a strong force to part with. It's not intentional it is just pure. Distance has a way of allowing things to flow effortlessly. It allows space for understanding and room for individuality.

In every social environment there is hierarchy. That's how it works, otherwise there is no guide for those who join the social environment to follow. I was unaware of that. I was genuinely uninterested in those things. One of the perks of being a DJ was that I bypassed all lines. Most times an event was held, the line for entry would be wrapped around the corner but there'd be no one inside. This was all for show. But for who?

Those moments of bypassing club lines and the reactions I'd receive to my oblivion of the status quo recall the film, The Truman Show. Everything is just right but something feels off. There's a subtle script that everyone follows. And when I poke around I begin to see the taped edges of this fabrication. Everyone is in on the joke and you can feel it. But no one will break character to admit it.

Building Cereal & Such was an experiment. It was done out of a genuine desire to have a space to work on my new record label, Good Posture. It was a shack in the back of a retail store. There was no sign and no marquee. The entry was through the back door of the retail shop, if you were curious enough to peer back and look you'd find us. Many would peek in and quickly turn back. They needed to be sold on it and I wasn't interested in convincing. I was interested in curiosity.

It was 3 years of building this concept. And it was time to make cereal a reality. I launched Cereal & Such with the aim to make a cereal that incorporated quality ingredients and tasteful design. It takes creating something to learn about yourself, because it's a reflection of you and the decisions you make.

As I struggled to accept things about myself it reflected in the company. Many people knew Cereal & Such as a company led by several people but it was solely me. I was afraid to admit that. When I began making music I wanted to be apart of a group and those feeling returned when starting this company. I had not yet realized that I was attempting to recreate the world in which I grew up eating cereal. It was home I attempting to bring with me and the journey in making Cinnamon Squares revealed that this was the manifestation of my family. My cereal *was* the group.

These experiences allowed me to reach the realization that it wasn't the environment that was flawed but the ideals I placed upon them. The relationships fostered were likely a figment of our imaginations. And upon realizing that came a natural and quiet withdrawal. Perhaps this all was by design.

That realization is a quiet one because you understand that it is your own conditioning that drives you to do these things. When I understood, that with all I knew, I could be led astray by my own mind, the views I held of others quickly faded.

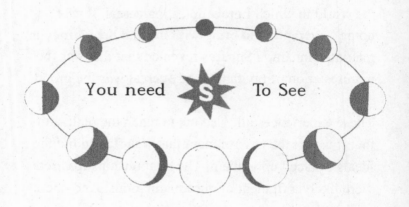

You need **S** To See

MIRACLES BY THE MILE

Living on my own was a dream come true, but even
that came with its own problems. I began to see a
pattern in behavior in the world around me. At work,
at the grocery' store, in my apartment building. The
behaviors varied but each recall a sinking feeling in
my stomach. It recall the feeling of catching my
Father on a bad day. But this wasn't my father, these
were my neighbors, my co-workers and friends. A
mentally unstable neighbor I would usher to his
apartment as he'd wander the hallways making a
ruckus. He was without a family of his own and he
expressed that to the rest of the tenants. The world
wasn't what I believed it to be and it was in my studio
apartment that I witnessed the onslaught of life's
unwavering stress on everyone. The causes of stress
are dependent upon the individual but its effects are
the same. Stress chips away at the fabric of a human
like the tide of the sea softens a stone. Wave after
wave after wave after wave. You learn to live with it
they say, you take the good with the bad. But it all
looked bad from where I was standing. What was
good about something if it was bad the next moment?

True, it may be life for many but this was not the life I sought. If it meant leaving the good and the bad behind all together it was worth my very own life. I naturally became quiet as a result of understanding how deep this sickness ran. I now understood why my Father kept a bottle of E&J beside his living room chair. I understood why petty arguments between strangers at the supermarket occurred, why violence ensues and our response is to share it. We are obsessed. Our eyes are transfixed. The sadness I sought to save my family from was what drove me from home. But was it my family who was sad or was it my response to what I saw? If this wasn't my sadness why I was driven to fix it? I was the product of suffering and I mimicked its symptoms. I had to understand why.

SPACE TO SEE

I grew up the second of five children. We were each incredibly close, artistic and held our uniquenesses. My Mother was hellbent on forging strong family ties and my Father would often retort his noted phrase when comparisons between school friends and siblings were made: "you have no friends". I was curious about the world, not home.

I believed I already understood my family, what more do I need to know? Naturally, we are blind to the things that are closest to us. I moved to Los Angeles for two reasons: it was far from my family and it was warm. I wanted the freedom to explore my curiosity without the threat of a sibling barging into my bedroom. I wanted my own experiences as an individual. I needed space to see things clearly.

After 5 years away I began to scratch the surface on these questions. I recently launched my cereal bar and was hired as a creative director at Apple. I had no idea what the role consisted of but this was a chance of a life time. My younger Sister had just graduated from college and would frequently bring up moving to Los Angeles. I knew my time of exploration was limited and I knew that because of how close a family we were. I spent a lot of time in New York because my elder Sister lived there and the familiarity gave comfort to my frequent trips. So if my younger Sister wanted to move to Los Angeles I would not deny her the experience. She moved and we shared my studio apartment. My deal was: a two month stay and then you have to find your space. Like any sibling she resented the proposal but accepted. I knew she would be fine.

We shared a similar bold spirit and this was an opportunity to see it for herself. After two months she went on her way and I had my space back, but something felt different. I sensed that this phase of careful experimentation was over.

FLOWS

I learned the nuances of songwriting after moving to Los Angeles. Prior to that my approach was to write on my own and then record over a pre-made beat I got from a producer. My songs sounded rigid. My voice strained from improper use, not the feeling I sought when I made music. It became tiresome and I began to realize this style didn't come natural to me. I began to riff over instrumentals as a way to allow the feeling to dictate what I was attempting to say. They weren't actual words but they included subtle random phrases. This was the start of transcribing my feelings into words. It brought me deeper into my process as a songwriter but it also allowed me to accept what came natural to me.

Years later I was approached outside of a supermarket by a music producer. He was the associate of a very popular music artist. He expressed that the artist was releasing an album in 24 hours and there were parts of his song that were unfinished. He expressed that the artist was releasing an album in 24 hours and there were parts of his song that were unfinished and asked if I could write the remainder of the song's verse. I obliged. This was an artist whom I admired and the opportunity to contribute to their work would be exciting. I agreed and told him to send me necessary files and I'd get to work. "I need the lyrics now", he stated hurriedly. "Now?", I asked, grocery bags still in hand. He quickly retorted, "Yea, I can play you the song now". We walked over to a nearby bench as he trailed beside me playing the song's instrumental from his phone. I jotted whatever I felt from the instrumental onto his notes app and handed him his phone. He expressed his thanks and scurried off. The following morning the album went live as he said. I listened to the song and every one my words landed. Even the riffs.

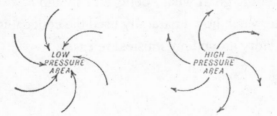

LONDON

Before arriving to the United States my Mother lived
in the United Kingdom. She and her sister attended
University in London. It was place I longed to be,
coupled with a semblance of my mothers former life
and a longing to travel. London is where the idea for
Good Posture had formed.

It was time to let go of what I believed I was in
exchange for what I genuinely felt. I was terrified of
no longer being known as an aspiring rapper. Rapping
was the only skill I could presently offer, though in
my songs you could hear the effect of my musical
influences in my cadence and delivery. It was time to
grow.

I didn't know Good Posture would be a record label
but by letting go of what I believed I should be I
began to watch how I naturally used the concept to
build a story around my musical releases.

My first collection accompanied music I wrote and produced during my stay in London. Life has taught me to truly understand the thing I loved the most, Music. To understand what I wanted from it and why. It shifted my attention in the direction of building my companies which, in building, have forced me to ask myself questions I would have never asked before. Music is simply music. If I needed it to change my life in order for me to enjoy it then it was not the love I claimed it was. With that experience I built an ecosystem to systematize it and a knowing to be free to enjoy this thing I loved so dearly.

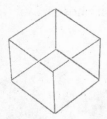 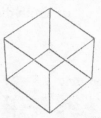

WHEN IT SPEAKS

The Truth speaks softly.
When it spoke it's softness would be frighten me.
I've heard the voice of that feeling forever and I can't
pinpoint its sound, but I know when I hear it.

When pain would come calling it spoke even softer.
It didn't interrupt and it didn't go out of it's way.
And that because it Is.
It is always there because it is all there is.
It spoke in my Father's practicality and it was the
source of my Mother's devotion.
I saw the effect it had on others when I tapped into it.

I'd use methods to disguise its origin, ashamed of
owning the weight of this thing. But the sweet scent
of Truth did as it chose.

REFINING MY UNDERSTANDING

Most of us don't know what we want. Often, we have a semblance of an idea and that idea is usually crowd sourced, contaminated by biases and opinions. So how do you know what you want from what you don't want? You know through experience. For most of my life I thought I wanted fame and I thought that because of the performers I watched on television. They danced and moved freely, they wore colorful garments and sung in unique ways. After touring and performing I realized I wasn't fulfilled. Following that tour, I began to examine each of my experiences with a cautioned view. I may have not known exactly what I was looking for but I knew what I did not want. There was no point in committing to anything if I had doubts, if I wasn't fully committed my attention would eventually wane. I knew if I felt the urgency then perhaps what I was looking for should in some way be presently accessible. How could it not? It took a while to understand that I simply wanted the freedom I saw the artists on stage with. That's what I wanted. It took time to refine what it is I was looking to say. That requires a great deal of openness. You don't arrive at that understanding with a fixed perspective. You learn to lean on what you find to be presently true.

Noise interrupts the natural process of curiosity and inspiration, be it your own mental noise or the mental noise of another that you internalize. I think of signal to noise ratio when I think of this particular time in my life. The signal is always transmitting, but it depends upon the level of noise in the environment you are in for you to hear it. I enjoy performing and touring when I want to do them. If I have to do them for any reason other than a natural desire then it becomes a job and I can get those anywhere.

WHAT COMES NATURAL

I never considered writing a memoir, likely because I long held a belief that writing would label me boring. I don't recall imbibing that belief but it is the only reason I've denied myself of writing. When you're in school reading and writing is the last thing you want to be known for so I quickly sought other interests, but when I purchased music I would always look for the credits. I knew the personnel involved in whatever I consumed and I followed their personal work as well. It became a web of sorts. Same approach with films, TV shows, product and clothing designers. Anything that came within reach I wanted to know it, beyond the cosmetics. That obsession to know has led me to the source of the obsession itself: me.

Writing this memoir helped write my album. For the space and sparseness the album provides, the self examinations in this book run deep. I began to reduce lyrics on a song until I was left with just a handful. "Just a Moment", the first song on my album is an example of that. I had nothing else to say other than what was said.

I enjoy the simplification of words, too many of them cloud ones mind. As I think back on my discography it has been an arrival to this point. Less and less words. More focus on the feeling and what It says and less of what I need to say.

Scan To Listen To
"Just A Moment"

FEAR

Fear is powerful motivator. It is the driving force behind most of our decisions. It's the ending cause of a relationship and the basis for beginning another. However, fear can be useful, it all depends on where you point it. I pointed mine towards what I feared most: not understanding who I was. I fear that far more than I fear of failure. Failure is relative. Most conflate failure with public humiliation and the idea of the public laughing at my failure wasn't scary. After they laugh then what happens? The initial sting may cause pain but that's short lived.

I used that fear as a ship to brave the seas of launching a business. I used it as barometer to measure the effect a relationship was having on me. I used it to move across the country on a whim because the opportune moment was fleeting. I used it to heighten the trust in my instincts. When you fear something what you fear is your reaction *to* the thing, not the thing itself. When you know you are being thrown a surprise party it's not the surprise you're afraid of, it's how you'll react to the surprise that scares you. I feared all the possibilities I would miss because of fear and I simply could not accept that.

My energy was best spent understanding why I was fearful, because if I understood why I felt fear then I would no longer be affected by it. A scary movie may be scary on your first watch but not on your fourth. Examining my fears led to many breakthroughs. There were no bogeyman's in any closet and the quicker I explored them the freer I became. It is there I realized I was playing a different game than my peers. The industry I was in was not the industry I was impacting. There was something beneath the surface and my weapon of choice was pointing in that direction.

Who is our greatest enemy? Ourselves. Who we believe ourselves to be, who we "think" we are and where we "should" be in life. Phrases like, "I am my own worst enemy" or, "I'm getting in my own way" have become commonplace to say, but what is said is the truth. And until that is explored and examined your search for the enemy will continue while you remain unaware that it has been you all along.

PLAYING THE GAME

In any game the winners are those who Understand
how It works.
To suffer on account of the game is to not Understand
It.

In order to Understand how something works an
individual must be willing to let go of what they
believe it to be in exchange for what it Is.
How do you know what you believe to be true and
what Is True?

You know by testing It.
Testing requires immersion.
Within immersion the exchange between what you
believe to be true and what is True is revealed.
Immersion is the Key for the door of Understanding.

To Understand the Game you have to immerse
yourself into the Game.
It is the only way one can test what they believe to be
true.

The quality of ones immersion into the game
Is the quality of ones desire to Understand the Game.

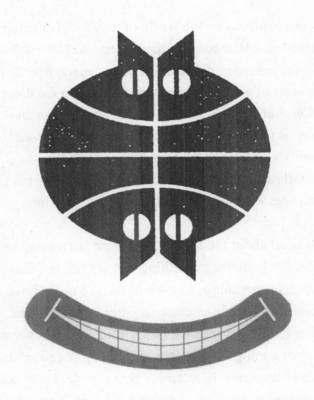

I KNOW WHERE IT COMES FROM

I was enamored by the world of artistry. Animated series and TV sitcoms, music videos and live shows, I was engrossed in every detail of it. I made friends on the basis of a collective feeling we shared for these artists, but we couldn't figure out what it was that drew us to them. Was it the equipment they used? Their style? Maybe the way they spoke? We assimilated on the basis of finding an answer, but the truth was we hadn't formed a specific question.

It was all about the feeling. We were attempting to collectively define something that we felt but those feelings were unique to each of us. We could bask in a shared feeling but an understanding of that had to occur first, otherwise we're saying things for the sake of saying things. And often, the saying is enough to give a semblance of attempts being made. I was not interested in attempts, I wanted to know. The varying degrees of difference soon made clear that it was artistic expression. An expression unique to each artist, each to their given ability to express. I now understand the distinct motif that I would see reoccurring in an artists' work. It's natural to them, like the stripes on a Zebra or spots on a Dalmatian.

Perhaps it's not something any artist is fully aware of but it's beautiful to the see the distinct patterns they've left for us to interpret. I began to understand that and as my question became clearer I naturally began to shift away from this group.

A SILENT EXCHANGE

I began dating a woman after my stay in London. I flew to meet her for the first time as we spent much time talking via social media. She was beautiful and I was enamored by the attention she gave me. On the surface it seemed we share many similarities. It was refreshing to meet a kindred spirit. I immediately flew to meet her and we spent a weekend together and began dating shortly after. Over the course of months I came to understand that she was a victim of a violent event, and through our time together I was hellbent on becoming a symbol of reliability, strength and support. I was determined to be that. The cracks in the pavement began to show shortly after but because of the promise I held to myself I refused to see it. I often found myself asking my friends and family what they thought of the situation.

I had a hard time with this role, it became tiresome to maintain this image. I did not like the weight that I bore. This self conflict I had to explore, because as long as I did not I would never understand what drove me uphold this ideal to begin with.

We lived very separate lives. We spoke infrequently and when we did see one another it was fragmented by the lack of openness. Mine, my failure to see what this really was and hers, the fear of admitting what it was: this was an exchange. A quiet and unspoken exchange. I was to be exactly who I believed myself to be and she was to be the beneficiary.

My mind worked in overdrive to rationalize and intellectualize what I was undoubtedly feeling. For the restrained oomph of truth I felt, the mind quickly followed with incessant chatter. I began to realize that there was something beneath the surface and I wasn't sure what. For as long as I knew of abuse I didn't believe that I had ever experienced it. But I have. We have committed violence against each other since the dawn of time. It is beyond domestic and physical abuse, but in the abuse of power, the misuse of control, of unauthorized give and take.

Everyone has experienced abuse in one form or another. And that is true because everyone, in one way or another, is a product of it. I was determined to win this relationship and I would do whatever was necessary to see it through. In the knowing of the violent event that had occurred I was present through the procession that followed. I attended court hearings and gave counsel when asked. I was determined to ensure it was saw through. This was the one hurdle we needed to jump through and once clear we would live our life together. But as time progressed the urgency of this matter began to change form. It was no longer the pressing issue. Her focus shifted towards the support of an artist's career she was aligned with. Money is to be made, I rationalized, but the oomph of truth was silent this time.

The ideals you hold are not your own, they are internalized by way of conditioning. The mind has collected every image, face, object and sound bite that you have laid your eyes and ears upon and with that has constructed a fabricated identity.

It is an intellectual holding cell. What I believed I wanted was not what I wanted. I wanted freedom. Freedom to be. And instead I sought out bondage.

Attachment is what I knew because it's all I saw. The cries of wanting out with actions that said the opposite. The thrill of the chase and the lull of the catch. It was a bark without a bite; a respite from loneliness. A complaint for complaints sake. It is all a game, a game we play with ourselves. Locked within the bondage of need pretending we are free. The suffering arose because I knew better, but I did not know why. Not yet.

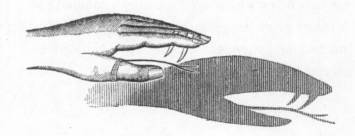

All relationships are built upon an exchange. Emotional or not a there is always a trade-off, so it's best to deal those cards openly, that way you can enjoy the very thing you are seeking through the relationship. Without that understanding you are playing a game of chance. A game of possibility. I was not interested in chance nor possibility I needed to know the basis of this exchange, but to do that meant I had to first accept it was an exchange. The relationship held great to importance to me. I cared deeply for this woman and I considered her my friend, but I was blinded by my own ignorance, by my egoic ideals of who I believed I should be. I was driven by the need to reach a goal that had no end. I did not see the reality of this situation. This was someone who was deeply suffering. This was not a scratched knee, this was an internal bleeding. Trauma is not something you solve in one sitting. It is a journey that requires changes to an individuals social environment and a complete divorce of a former life. It requires a death of sorts.

I liken the experience of this relationship to being led through a series of rooms and corridors inside a large mansion. It was a chase and my focus was on the catch, so much so that I became unaware of very clear patterns. I *have* been in this room before and this is not a large mansion. It takes time to see things as they are, conditioning is too strong. The mind has gargantuan faculties. The set changes of its fabrication are too elaborate to not consider for a moment its validity. And that's all it needs. Just a moment and it's got you. After many tumultuous events I begun to see things as they were and not as I imagined. The construct was beginning to glitch and I began to understand what triggered it. Pain. Pain brought the mind to its knees. Pain is immediate, it is real. It is not abstract. The mind is not real, it lives in abstraction. It was about time to leave and I could feel it. I pulled in the aide of a therapist who specialized in trauma research because I needed to understand what I was facing. The side effects of co-dependency rival that of an opium. My partner could feel the changes as well. I was no longer reactive to her outbursts or long disappearances. I understood what was happening, I could now recognize the subtle accent marks of each room and each corridor.

It was time to go and when the moment would present itself I would do as it asked. On my way out I saw another gentleman entering the home. He was in awe like I was once before. It was time, my stop had arrived.

OFFICE & GALLERY

I was opening an office. I titled it Office and Gallery because deep inside I knew I hadn't arrived yet. It was another exercise to understand exactly what I was doing. Opening my office was one of the hardest things I've done up until that point. And it wasn't the construction that was hard. It wasn't finding the building either, that stuff came easy. The stress was what the effects of this decision were doing to my mind. As I drove an hour to the leasing office to drop off my deposit every fiber in my body was at war. I had all of this money and I was going to use it to open an office? What am I doing? Again I knew this was easy. I had plenty experience in this and I knew what I was doing, but the battle was in my mind. It was looking for any escape from this. I signed the lease and returned to my car. This was yet another exercise in my artistry.

I had questions that I need answered
I had symptoms that I need canceled
Took a journey I'm a journey man
Took the long way home then

Take the back roads and alleyways
See it through just to end the pain
Gain the clarity and peace of mind
So you never have to leave again

Make the money work like magic
Got a bad hand that's tragic
I be in the cut with no tint
Wait up who you talking on the phone with?
Truth is..
I be out residing where the Truth is
Truth is..
I be out residing where the Truth is

WHERE YOU'LL FIND ME

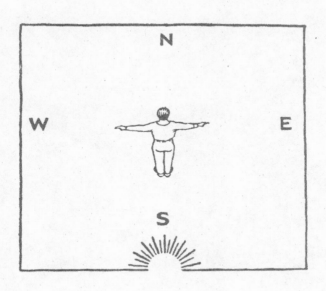

Scan To Listen To
"Where You"ll Find Me"

THE FINAL FRONTIER

I view each of these experiences as an astronaut navigating an uncharted dimension in search of an undiscovered planet. With boosters attached to my rocket ship I bear the added weight with an understanding that under great pressure what is true will emerge, with any excess falling to the wayside. It may feel like a burden to carry but it is the only chance you have for an arrival of any sort. While the destination is my own the journey was to be shared. Some, there to test the true willingness to reach my destination, others, mildly curious, looking to buy time for a moments resolve from loneliness.

You learn as you go if you want to own the experience and gain peace of mind. No one is going where you are going. Some are looking to hitch a ride towards your general direction and some are looking for an escape. Regardless of these choices the journey is the journey and these were chances I was willing to take. What else was there for me to do? It would be a mere excuse as to why I could not. I had nothing to lose and I knew that. I could not fathom a life wondering of the possibilities. This was the final frontier and I felt that deep within my bones.

My family flew in for the Holidays. It was the first time the entire family was under one roof in nearly 5 years. In between the festivities my Mother pulled me aside and asked how I've been feeling, she was aware I just launched my cereal and she saw I was quiet. I told her I wasn't sure but I felt a shift was near. "You will know", she replied softly. I quietly nodded back. We continued to enjoy the remainder of the holiday festivities. The following day I saw my family off to the airport and decided to head to my office. There was something I needed to see.

I approached the doors of my building, unlocked the gate and stood at the entryway for a moment. Peering through the glass entrance I looked at every square inch of this rectangle that I rebuilt from scratch. I saw the products I made that sat in the window. I saw boxes of Cereal & Such packaged on a nearby shelf. I looked over at the custom hanging racks I built to hold my clothes. It became suddenly clear what was happening and the weight of this realization stunned every fiber in my body. I was all of the things that I came here to pursue and it stood right in front of me. I had put it on full display for the world to see, but that recognition was solely for my eyes.

In my endless chase a thin veil obscure my vision, but I could no longer unsee what I now saw very clearly.

The journey has begun with a sincere desire to know the Truth. The truth about who I am. There has been favor in my genuine curiosity to understand and in that has brought relative ease along the way. I have made an exchange in what I believed things to be for what they truly were. It was the cost of the journey and I was happy to pay. Even when presented with great risk of danger the path always provided an alternate way. There were larger forces at work and I was certain of it this time.

"So, what's next? Are we done doing each of these things? Are we sure? Perhaps there's another opportunity to explore". My mind, in its insatiable appetite for pleasure, searching for any reason to continue with the chase. I offer no response and continued my gaze. My phone began to ring, it was my mother. "Hey, we are in Las Vegas. Your Dad mistakenly bought our return flight to LAS. We are fixing it now". I smiled and ended the call. Unlocking the front door I walked into my office and quietly nodded to myself. It was time to go.

FREEDOM

What I sought from this life was Freedom.
Freedom that my Mother & Father have given me.
The Freedom that sits in plain sight.
So plain that it is quickly mistaken.
Freedom that needs no convincing.
Freedom that is won in total & utter surrender.
Freedom that I have already had.

This album is my declaration of Freedom.

Scan To Listen To My Self Titled Debut Album

WWW.THEOMARTINS.ORG

IT'S RIGHT WHERE YOU LEFT IT